I Love Horses

Clydesdales

Maria Koran

AV2
www.av2books.com

Step 1
Go to **www.av2books.com**

Step 2
Enter this unique code
ULQFJ2DRE

Step 3
Explore your interactive eBook!

AV2 is optimized for use on any device

Your interactive eBook comes with...

Read

Audio
Listen to the entire book read aloud

Videos
Watch informative video clips

Weblinks
Gain additional information for research

Try This!
Complete activities and hands-on experiments

Key Words
Study vocabulary, and complete a matching word activity

Quizzes
Test your knowledge

Slideshows
View images and captions

View new titles and product videos at www.av2books.com

Clydesdales

CONTENTS

Clydesdales are big horses. They are known for their strength.

Clydesdales come from Scotland.

FIVE POINT
CLYDESDALES

Clydesdales are some of the heaviest horses. They have long hairs on their legs. These are called feathers.

A Clydesdale’s hoof is about the size of a dinner plate.

Clydesdales have thick manes and coats.

Most Clydesdales are brown. Parts of their heads and legs are white.

Clydesdales are known as "gentle giants." They are calm horses.

Clydesdales are also very hard workers.

Many Clydesdales work on farms. They help farmers plow fields. Clydesdales also pull heavy tools.

A team of Clydesdales can plow about 2 acres (0.8 hectares) in a day.

Baby Clydesdales are called foals. They grow quickly.

Clydesdales become adults after four years.

A Clydesdale foal gains about 4 pounds (2 kilograms) of weight each day.

Clydesdales are a mix of different horses.

They came from farming horses and the horses that knights rode.

People in cities liked Clydesdales.

They started using them to pull carriages and wagons.

Scotland used to have many Clydesdales. Today, there are not many left.

Most Clydesdales now live in North America.

See what you have learned about Clydesdales.

Which of these pictures show Clydesdales?

KEY WORDS

Research has shown that as much as 65 percent of all written material published in English is made up of 300 words. These 300 words cannot be taught using pictures or learned by sounding them out. They must be recognized by sight. This book contains 52 common sight words to help young readers improve their reading fluency and comprehension. This book also teaches young readers several important content words, such as proper nouns. These words are paired with pictures to aid in learning and improve understanding.

Page	Sight Words First Appearance
4	are, big, come, for, from, their, they
7	a, about, have, is, long, of, on, some, the, these
8	and, faces, most, parts, white
11	also, as, hard, very
12	can, day, farms, help, in, many, work
15	after, each, four, grow, years
16	came, different, that
18	people, liked
19	started, them, to
21	America, left, live, not, now, there

Page	Content Words First Appearance
4	Clydesdales, horses, Scotland
7	dinner plate, feathers, hairs, hoof, legs
8	coats, manes
11	"gentle giants," workers
12	acres, farmers, fields, team, tools
15	adults, foals, pounds, weight
16	knights
18	cities
19	carriages, wagons
21	North America

Published by AV2
350 5th Avenue, 59th Floor New York, NY 10118
Website: www.av2books.com

Library of Congress Control Number: 2019954938

ISBN 978-1-7911-1955-3 (hardcover)
ISBN 978-1-7911-1956-0 (softcover)
ISBN 978-1-7911-1957-7 (multi-user eBook)
ISBN 978-1-7911-1958-4 (single-user eBook)

Printed in Guangzhou, China
1 2 3 4 5 6 7 8 9 0 24 23 22 21 20

022020
100919

Project Coordinator: John Willis Art Director: Terry Paulhus

AV2 acknowledges Alamy, Getty, iStock, Minden Pictures, and Shutterstock as the primary image suppliers for this title.